CHOOSE
to be
INCREDIBLE

VICTORIA REI

Get More from **LIFE** – Make **SHIFT** Happen

Printed in the United States of America.

Editing by Joanne Shwed, Backspace ink (www.backspaceink.com)

"Find and follow the Good," "Stand Firm until Shift Happens," "Success IQ = Emotional IQ + Social IQ," and "Being My Own Hero" are registered trademarks.

Case history names have been changed to preserve anonymity.

Published by Rei and Associates, LLC

ISBN-10: 0-9899474-0-8
ISBN-13: 978-0-9899474-0-4

Dedication

For Augie, my dear husband, who gives me the wonder of being cherished with devotion and showed me what it is to be really loved.

To my daughters, Elizabeth and Jaclyn, I'm so honored to be your mother.

All of you are the joys of my life. Thank you for being who you are.

"*Our deepest fear is not that we are inadequate, our deepest fear is that we are powerful beyond measure. It is our light, not our darkness that most frightens us. ... Your playing small does not serve the world. There is nothing enlightened about shrinking so that other people won't feel insecure around you. We were born to make manifest the glory of God that is within us. ... in everyone. And as we let our own light shine, we unconsciously give other people permission to do the same. As we are liberated from our own fear, our presence automatically liberates others.*"

—Marianne Williamson

Acknowledgements

I would like to acknowledge all the mentors who helped shape my awakening to the realization—both directly and indirectly—i.e., "I am at Choice": Marilyn Attebury, Andrea Lambert, Al-Anon, Adult Children of Alcoholics, Don McKinnon, Mark E. Furman, and SAGE participants Steve, Penelope, Gloria, Don, and Les.

Teachers and authors have also influenced me with their journeys and discoveries. Many thanks to their willingness to share their lessons and conclusions with the world: Daniel Goleman, Wayne Dyer, Oprah Winfrey, Marianne Williamson, Debbie Ford, John Bradshaw, Elizabeth Kübler-Ross, Barbara De Angelis, John Gray, Ellen Kreidman, Tony Robbins, Jack Canfield, Mark Victor Hansen, Bob Proctor, Dan Baker, Sam Horn and Stephen Covey, Sr. and Jr.

Personal development weekends have given me the experience of awakening more and more to who I really am: Transactional analysis studies, SAGE, Avatar Course, Self-Awareness Institute seminar and Brain Power On training.

Finally, to my editor, Joanne Shwed, thank you for tak-

ing care of the details and your much needed assistance.

Of course, to Ann McIndoo, my author's coach, and Mishael, manuscript coordinator.

Thank you all, from the depth of my heart.

Contents

INTRODUCTION

"Self-trust is the first secret of success."

—Ralph Waldo Emerson

Although I left behind my childhood of abuse long ago, I am led to share my story as a way to encourage others to find and choose a path to well-being no matter what obstacles may be in the way. To have resilience and continue choosing to "find and follow the Good" (i.e., look for teachings of good and constructively useful models from which we can learn and follow) require faith and courage to get to the finish line of what you want in your life. Anyone who chooses to be the best he or she can be contributes to him or herself as well as many others. The gifts we give ourselves in the process are also given to others, along the way, knowingly and unknowingly.

Deciding to "Be Your Own Hero"™ and choosing to develop high emotional and social skills make your life easier. These decisions and choices get you from striving to thriving and from chaos to peace.

When your toolbox is full of effective tools to help you deal with badly behaving people, or your own internal processing of emotions, you can become more effective in your job, with your life purpose and in living your life. Your life, family and friends will show up, giving you more of what you want.

Nourishing relationships have a beneficial impact on our health; toxic ones can act like slow poison in our bodies. When you choose better health and relationships, you will be better for your choices and add to the "hundredth monkey effect" (i.e., critical mass). In other words, when enough people do the same, it becomes the norm; then, society changes to follow the new norm.

There is a song by Bobby McFerrin called "Don't Worry, Be Happy." When we get to the critical mass number of people who CHOOSE To Be Happy and have the skills to do so, sustainably- we will all solve the local and global problems we face synergistically and with amazing outcomes.

Will you do your part?

CHOOSE To Be Happy.

Choose gifts of change to well-being.

Choose and define success in any way you want to do, be and have a better life. Add to the critical mass buildup, leading to a better world, right where you are now.

Choose to be Incredible!

CHAPTER ONE

WHO CAN I BE AGAINST THESE ODDS?

"If one advances confidently in the direction of his dreams, and endeavors to live the life which he has imagined, he will meet with a success unexpected in common hours."

—Henry David Thoreau

I awoke abruptly from a deep sleep. I was yanked out of bed by my hair, dragged across the floor and downstairs to a bathroom, and forced to eat dog food from a dish on the floor like a dog. This was a lesson from my mother. Apparently, I had forgotten to feed the dog the night before. It was really my sister's chore, but she forgot. I was the oldest kid, so I was "responsible" for everyone doing their chores and behaving in our household; now, I was given "a lesson."

Another time, my two sisters (ages five and seven) and I (age nine) were left alone in the house. We were being punished for not getting enough packing done for our move in two days. We were left on our own overnight without supper or food so we could get "the packing done."

During that evening, distracting ourselves from the outside darkness and being alone, we found letters in

9

boxes from which we discovered that we had different fathers and, unbeknownst to us, different last names. Mother had lied to each of us about the identity of our fathers. Until that time, we all thought that we had the same father and that she was in the process of leaving yet another husband.

As time went on, we saw that she gave us the same last name of the current husband. Since we moved a lot, she was able to do this without legal process, even in school. This was the pattern we came to recognize as we grew older. She had seven husbands before she stopped marrying at about age 44; six of those marriages occurred prior to age 38. She was 20 years old when she bore me.

Growing up was like being in hostile territory, wondering when I would again be in harm's way of the explosive emotional and physical violence. Daily? Weekly? My mother was mentally ill and ran from—instead of to—treatment based on diagnosis, which could have and now does manage her type of mental illness fairly well. In spite of the episodes, I've come to realize and accept the skills I learned from my mother: cooking, cleaning, organizing, ironing, managing a home, problem solving, learning to be resourceful and practical and surviving in a primitive or civilized living environment.

While raising me and three other siblings, my mother's choices led to living in various types of homes: from a one-room log cabin in Alaska with cooking on a coal and wood stove and bathing in the creek, to an upper-middle-class, two-story home with a finished basement. I've lived in 17 cities in seven western U.S. states and three Asian countries, and then left home at 16. I attended public schools until my senior year in high school. I skipped tenth grade because we were in Okinawa and school cost too much there. Later, I found my way through undergraduate school and earned two graduate degrees. For better or worse, self-sufficiency was the legacy or inheritance I received from parentage.

What would lead a mother to treat her children so cruelly? What do children who have been raised under continued duress grow up to be like? What issues do they have to deal with to live life normally? How do they cope if they're always waiting for the ax to fall again suddenly, with predictable and unpredictable outbursts of rage, insane acting out and potential danger?

Can they have a normal life?

What do Children of Abuse learn about relationships, trust and love when life is so confusing? For
me, love showed up in untrustworthy environments
with a parent who was supposed to nurture me
(and maybe did sometimes). Then, just when it felt
safe—*WHAM*! A slap across the face, a grab of hair,
a head banged against the wall, a scalding pot of
coffee poured on my body, or my face stuffed in the
toilet again and again, near drowning until a step-
father pulled my mother off of me.

It is similar to being a war hostage. The parent or
parents are the enemy from whom to escape, but
how? We were so little and still needed to depend on
our parents to survive. One of the hard parts is that
our abusive parent looks and acts normal to others
outside of the home. No one knew and who would
we tell? Who would listen? We were just kids. Even
if we did find someone to tell, who would believe
us? The abusive parent would cover up, when or if
confronted, and then take us back home and really
punish us even more, in privacy and away from anyone to see. The parent threatened us with even more
harm if we told—especially at school, where scars

and welts were visible and some kind of explanation was required.

In third grade, I was taken to the principal's office more than once with welts on my face and the side of my head where Mother had whipped me with an electric frying pan cord and the hardware on the end of it, which created a visible black-and- blue knot on the side of my head. I had been severely instructed to lie and say, "I fell down the stairs at our house," but we did not even have any stairs!

When the principal asked me how I got this bruise, I lied like I had been forewarned because I did not believe that he could protect me. Even if he did, for a time, I did not want my sisters and me to go to a foster home, which was not a trustworthy option from the stories we had heard. The principal's reaction was one of reluctant surrender as there was nothing he could do about a report of a "fall."

As I became an adult and went to college, I learned that I was not alone in feeling isolated, resulting from this type of childhood abuse. I wondered: how much does this happen in our country? Is this a minor issue? Why didn't other family members intervene and do something to protect us? The answers I found led to an understanding that parental abuse usually comes from parents who are self-abusing alcohol and/or drugs; about one-half of that population is mentally ill without diagnosis or treatment. Over time, this behavior worsens the illness and compounds damages by 400% or more (national Council on alcoholism and drug dependence, Inc. (NCADD)).

About one-half of both populations are part of a group called "dual diagnosis" (i.e., those who are plagued with untreated mental illness and are self-medicating with alcohol and/or drugs). My mother drank later in her life. Self-medicating is more destructive in the longer run, but it numbs immediate problems and is used as a way to cope with emotions and life by the consumer.

There are now organizations that help educate and provide resources for the addict and/or the mentally ill consumer, and educational resources for the spouses and family of those with these illnesses: 12-step programs of Alcoholics Anonymous and Al-Anon, NCADD, and the National Alliance on Mental Illness (NAMI).

However, the only organization I'm aware of that addresses the effects of abuse on children, even as they become adults, is adult Children of Alcoholics (ACA). This organization identifies the emotional "war wounds" and posttraumatic stress disorder (PTSD) effects left behind when growing up in this kind of environment. development of out-of-control self-reliance, resulting from a lack of proper nurturing from parent caretaking, is one of the characteristics of adult children of abuse (Oliver Diaz, 1988).

There are more deaths and disabilities each year in the United States from substance abuse than from any other cause. More than half of all adults have a family history of alcoholism or problem drinking, adult children of alcoholism and/or abuse. More than nine million children live with a parent who is dependent on alcohol and/or illicit drugs. About 18 million Americans have alcohol problems. About five to six million Americans have drug problems (NCADD).

When I interned at the NCADD, we learned that, for every addiction abuser, there are four to five significant family members, including children, who are deeply affected in their lives (NCADD). If you multiply 24 million times four to five, we're looking at 100 million to 122 million people in this country who are deeply affected by alcohol and drug addicts. That's about half of our population! Mental illnesses include major depression, schizophrenia, bipolar disorder, obsessive-compulsive disorder, panic disorder, PTSD and borderline personality disorder.

One in four—25%, or approximately 58 million Americans—experience a mental health disorder in a given year. The World Health Organization has reported that four of ten leading causes of disability in the United States and in other developed countries are mental disorders. By 2020, major depressive illness will be the leading cause of disability in the world for women and children (NAMI).

When all these statistics are added up, it appears that 75% of America is dealing with families that suffer with addiction and/or mental illness and experience dire effects on relationships and the emotional makeup of family members. Added to that estimate, only 10% to 15% of our population is truly emotionally healthy.

The good news is that Recovery is possible. Once these truths are recognized and faced. There are resources for recovery like Adult Children of (Abuse or) Alcoholism – ACA.

ACA points out that the result of trauma as a child of mentally ill parents, at the brunt of abuse and abandoned parenting, is PTSD. Those of us from ACA are the walking wounded until we face our grief, isolation and ardent self-reliance and self-sufficiency. This prevents us from asking for help since, as children, there was nowhere to get help. Most often, we enter into abusive or empty relationships and have a high need for perfectionism or a need to be right and in control. Survival traits are people pleasing, being invisible and/or submissive (ACA).

The statistics to which I just referred are staggering. Unless we *choose to improve our self- development*, dysfunctional relationships will continue to increase in our culture and society. Unless or until individuals take it upon themselves to recover emotionally and learn to do better than they were taught or experienced as children, dysfunctional and disconnected behavior in relationships will continue to be inherited. Dysfunction is now very common, and these illnesses are insidiously baffling for families.

When I was growing up, there was little information about the signs of these diseases and even less knowledge about how to handle a family member who was acting out in addiction or mental illness. Because of this lack of information, neither my mother's spouses, nor her parents, nor any other family or friends knew what to do with her behavior or about "saving" her children.

The pattern was to cope and adjust until it got so bad that you have to leave for self-preservation. No husband, family, or fatherly intervention took place because it was "too hard" to treat an ill person caught in these afflictions unless he or she volunteered for treatment. However, the addicted and/or mentally ill abuser is usually in denial of his or her behavior—and the impact of it—because they are consumed with their own focus and illness.

There is rarely voluntary treatment until the time that their actions lead to acute consequences with the law and institutions or their own death. By that time, the trail of trauma they have inflicted on others is great. The children, in my mind, are hurt the worst. They are left to try to figure out how to have healthy relationships and families without needed healthy modeling from their parents.

John Bradshaw, author of numerous books for children of alcoholics, developed the concept of choosing a healthy surrogate family based on recognizing and getting support for emotional recovery as children when we are adults. As a child, I watched other families in school and on TV (e.g., *Leave It To Beaver*, *Father Knows Best*, *The Waltons* and *Bonanza*) as examples for family modeling and healthy parenting. I sought self-help books and seminars as a young adult, particularly after having my own children. I wanted to break the cycle and not pass it on.

We Adult children who were abused , work to overcome these odds; however, in spite of them, we *learn* to more than cope with life. Some of us *learn* to embrace life, *recognize* the hurdles and break the cycle of dysfunction in our birth families by learning to become healthy and "well" ourselves. Then, we find and choose others who are higher functioning, which develops "well-being" support in our life journey.

In order to accomplish a better life for ourselves and our children, we must take the inner journey of emotional recovery and self-development, and learn emotional skills to problem solve on a much higher level than what we experienced growing up. We learn healthy social skills in order to develop better relationships than we had. Part of that process eventually leads to forgiving the abusive parent or parents, yet not continuing to submit to or tolerate abusive behavior from them or anyone else. Sooner or later, some of us decide to become well and search for ways in which to be emotionally healthy and raise our children in a much better environment than we had. We "find and follow the Good."

It is a slow process for women because our culture teaches us to give and nurture and it is part of our natural inclination; however, in our role of reversal upbringing by self-absorbed dysfunctional parenting, we were taught to overgive, be the parent in our family and not expect reciprocity. We were taught to be the responsible one in our family, at the expense of our childhood, while the parent was immature, irresponsible, abusive and abandoning. It's a challenge to learn to know how much to give, accept and receive reciprocity before giving more, and then expect to be treated well in relationships. Our choices and boundaries are poor, often leading to mistreatment and betrayal.

Smart Women, Foolish Choices (Cowan et al., 1986) offers insight into this dynamic. We set ourselves up for betrayal by not knowing how to choose others who are emotionally healthy to be our friends, mates and chosen family. We tend to rescue the needy in order to satisfy our habit of being needed and being the responsible caretaker. Learning healthy boundaries and better choices in relationships can be as hard, just as making healthier eating choices when we are emotional eaters. As with food, relating to others is necessary in order to live, but how do we do it with healthy outcomes and a healthy balance?

As Daniel Goleman points out in *Emotional Intelligence* (Goleman, 1995), children in schools are suffering more than ever from violence. Very low emotional and social skills are demonstrated for problem solving and conflict resolution. Teachers and leaders in these institutions and/or in the workplace do not know how to resolve or prevent this rapidly growing rate of violence and conflict.

Yet, in spite of the odds, some of us choose to change ourselves and lead a better life, than we had as children. We have found that, by changing ourselves, we become a change agent in our families and at work, and with our friends and community at large. By committing to wellness for ourselves, we become models and leaders in our everyday lives. By choosing the direction to well-being, we then choose to develop our emotional and social skills. That leads us to live a better life and overcome challenges in peaceful ways.

Questions for Thought:

1. What choices am I making in my life?

2. What is my life like—overall?

3. What do I want my life to be?

CHAPTER TWO

IS LIFE THIS HARD FOR EVERYONE?

"Being humble doesn't mean one has to be a mat."

—*Maya Angelou*

As a child, I remember questioning, "Why is this happening? How can it stop? When is it going to stop?" Once in a while, when I could play outside in the meadow next door, I'd lie in the tall, green grass and look up at the blue sky and fluffy clouds. I'd imagine pleasant possibilities, such as flying or resting on the clouds and feeling the cushy softness. I'd imagine alternate experiences— a healthy family life of fun-loving scenarios—so I could feel good. Imagining good family interactions helped me relax from the constant high-alert state of being I had to be in to survive inside my family and life in the house. For me, the high-alert danger place was at home; school was where I could relax and learn.

Now, though, many children are facing high alert at home and school. Bullying and violence is a major concern in public schools. Even the workplace tolls that 60% of employees feel or perceive they've been bullied at work (Thunderbird School of Global Management, Pearson, 2010).

Where can we be safe emotionally and physically? Where and with whom do we not have to be on high alert? More importantly, how can we convert the unsafe places and make them safe again?

Growing up as the oldest child, it seemed as if I had more responsibilities. I buffered Mother's anger and attention away from my younger sisters and brother by distracting her attention to me and placating her demands and/or reframing her focus. John Bradshaw calls this the role of "hero" (Bradshaw, 1990). This worked fairly well until I could no longer tolerate her abuse. I lived on my own at school, away from home, at age 16. When I left, my sisters got the brunt of Mother's abuse. Unfortunately, Mother's untreated mental illness got worse as she aged. The last of the siblings—my brother—got the worst, which damaged his life in significant ways.

Then, when I was 17 years old and home after graduating from high school, Mother came at me with a bottle of French's Worcestershire Sauce in order to smash my face in because I did not get Lea & Perrins. The grocery store had been out of that brand. Something snapped in me, and my power must have kicked in. I took her raised wrist with the "weapon" in it and looked her straight in the eye. As I was pushing her backwards, step by step to our third-floor open window, I told her that if she ever touched me again—or attempted to—I would push her out the window and watch her fall to the ground. Whatever rage or blackout place her mind went to snapped back, and the back of her thighs must have felt the windowsill press against them. She finally lowered her arms, and her eyes shifted as if she did not know what just happened.

I told her that I was moving out, and then rented a furnished room a few blocks away. I turned 18 years old a few months later, living on my own, walking to and from a new job. I had raised myself in spite of uncontrolled daily and weekly parental raging, physical violence and emotional traumatizing, and I was still intact.

I'm not sure how my sisters fared after I left. I had to be focused on surviving in a different way: how do I make money and support myself? My sisters and I have since shared some of our feelings and thoughts, but it is too painful for us to share our childhood experiences. When we talk now, we choose to talk about our current lives and children— safer subjects. We live in far corners of the country, so visits are infrequent.

My life became about working, going to college on my own and finding scholarships and financial assistance to do so. Apparently, being able to relax and feel safer at school than at home left an imprint on me. I liked learning and still do. I consider myself a seeker, which has led to lots of college and more than one graduate degree.

Eventually, dating and developing a relationship took place, yet I had no model or mentoring for choosing well or marrying a supportive mate. Watching those TV programs did not fill in the gaps about choosing relationships and creating healthy emotional intimacy. Being raised as the child as well as the parent taught me how to be responsible for others, but it did not teach me how to feel or care for my emotional well-being. The TV programs gave glimpses of what a happy family looked like and how they interacted with each other, but they didn't show me how to date or interact with someone and know who they really are.

Since Mother was the way she was, no other adult stayed around for very long, or she'd take off and move us again. Connection was not dependable with others; either we or they did not last long. Everything had been driven by fear. The stepfathers who came and went were either abusive in other ways or passive and helpless to restrain Mother and her behavior, so they left and left us behind with her.

Mother was always on "good behavior" during courtship and when the new husband was at home; however, as time went on, she lost control of her rages and spontaneous irrational behavior. Then, the husbands would leave. They had an option that we did not have as minors.

My fear at home was traded for survival and attempts to find my way in the world to a better place and life. Eventually, I learned what I wanted to know about myself in relationships. The learning and modeling came from books, counseling, education and group self-awareness seminars. Reading

included John Bradshaw's work on choosing a surrogate family, *Codependent No More* (Beattie, 1987)
and John Gray's works on male versus female thinking (*Men Are from Mars, Women Are from Venus,*
1992), Al-Anon and ACA meetings, and books on
reparenting myself (*The 12 Steps to Self-Parenting for
Adult Children* by Oliver Diaz (1988) and others).
Self-empowerment was obtained by releasing neg-
ative emotions during the Self-Awareness Institute
weekend seminar. Individual counseling and the
avatar Course (consciousness development training) and neuroscience/neuropath reprogramming
(Brain power on coaching with don Mckinnon)
also helped.

*I was determined to find out how to have a better and a
good life.* I became aware that I could *choose.* I knew
that I did not want to be like my mother. Eventually, I had daughters and knew that I wanted to be a
healthy parent—emotionally clear, authentic, happy
and carefree—and raise them well. I wanted to
make choices for a better life for me and for them.

The gift of my childhood (i.e., growing up as a codependent person, with a narcissistic, raging, manip-
ulative and controlling mother) is that I chose to

parent very differently. As a child, I was in a situation and coped as best as I could. The beauty is that, with a concentrated effort as an adult, I can choose to create a different experience for my children. By turning this tide, it positively impacts current and future generations.

Questions for Thought:

1. How can I choose to lead my life to be what I want?

2. Who do I want to be? What kind of person do I want to BE?

3. What affect do those around me have on me?

4. What effect do I have on others?

CHAPTER THREE

CAN LIFE GET BETTER?

"The worst prison would be a closed heart."

—*Pope John Paul II*

When I lay in the meadow, looking up at the sky and clouds, I often wondered and imagined what my life would be like in the future. I truly wanted a better life, and an emotionally free and good life. I imagined what it would be like to have parents who were loving, nurturing and protective, and who could be leaned on and take care of me. They would also love each other and show it.

I asked myself, "How and when can I have a better life? How could I be loved in a normal, healthy and demonstrated way?" Mother told us that she loved us, yet this same person would reign with terror and beat us in merciless ways. Is that love? It was very confusing.

Did love mean emotional and physical pain? Did

it mean betrayal and unexpected hostility? Intellectually, I knew this was not so, yet I had no other emotional experience. Could kindness be trusted when it could suddenly turn against me in a moment's notice without warning?

"Surely, when I'm old enough," I'd say to myself, "I'll not have to be around or deal with harmful people. Mother is an exception and other people don't do what she does to us."

I knew what I did *not* want.

After looking at other families during that time, it seemed as if our family was an exception to how life was normally lived. Other kids at school didn't seem to have problems at home. So, all I had to do was grow up and be on my own to have a good life, right? Well, when I grew up and lived on my own, I realized that there was a lot I did not know about myself, my feelings, or what I really wanted. My life had been about living in fear and constantly thinking about staying out of harm's way as much as possible. Relaxing and living life normally was a challenge.

I did not realize that I would face life and others unprepared because I did not have healthy parenting. Healthy emotional skills or social relationship skills were not taught to me or modeled for me. As I watched others, I realized that I needed these skills and had to learn them on my own. I knew this was missing, but where would I find out how to learn them?

The only way I knew how to learn these skills was in school, so I majored in psychology in undergraduate school. I studied child abuse and information on mental illness. I learned that abused children often become abusive adults. I was determined to break the cycle and not follow that pattern.

To do so, I took extra courses in communications, facilitating group dynamics, counseling techniques and transactional analysis (TA) (i.e., where parent-adult-child personas exist in all of us), and learned about stages of grieving resulting from change cycles. I wanted to understand people and myself—and maybe even my mother. Later, when I was discouraged about relationships and the losses and disappointments rather than the dependable love and nurturing that come from genuine love, I sought counseling and self-development training.

Al-Anon helped me learn about detachment. ACA helped me learn about self-parenting and the hypervigilant self-sufficiency pattern that abused children take into adulthood. That pattern interferes with allowing interdependence in a healthy relationship and/or prevents an adult child from recognizing and selecting a mate with the capacity for healthy love, which includes receiving.

How could I give and receive love, and know about being cherished with devotion, if I didn't give it to myself? How could I give and receive love if I didn't know how to receive goodness in my life? I could give very well and be a good parent, and nurture my children, but I still didn't know how to have a personal relationship, which included receiving dependable care and nurturing for me. I didn't know how to assess someone else's capacity for giving and receiving genuine, interactive love.

To get to that level, I learned that I needed to be able to attune to my feelings and to what I wanted, and use my "gut" to feel the energy reaction to any dynamic in interactions with others. The discovery was that the journey had to start with me tuning in to myself, to learn and recognize what I was feeling in the moment.

To do that, I had to clear out emotional scars and baggage, resentments, pent-up anger and rage, and then grief, relief, sadness and pain. The major breakthrough came from attending a Self-Awareness institute weekend seminar with Andrea Lambert. I learned that, until we can heal our inner child, we are not emotionally free, and we cannot interact with life and others freely.

To trust others, I had to trust myself.

Emotional baggage does not allow one's self to do that. Clearing out the baggage gives us freedom to know and trust one's self and one's feelings. To know what I'm feeling is the start to a relationship foundation; however, developing my healthy emotional management was necessary before successfully developing relationships.

I determined that I had a lot to learn and uncover about myself before I could become better than I was. I had to learn what I had not been taught while growing up about a healthy self, family and relationship skills. Fortunately, I learned that there were resources of books, thought leaders and seminars to uncover what I wanted and needed to learn. I wanted to be emotionally, spiritually, physically and financially healthy and thriving. I wanted to break my cycles of fear. I wanted to expect and experience happiness.

Questions for Thought:

1. What is the best life I can dream of for myself? What do I want in my life?

2. Am I happy, at least sometimes? What am I doing when I am?

3. What is love to me? Is it in my life? Is it healthy love?

4. Where can I find models of well-being around me?

CHAPTER FOUR

WHO AM I?

"Freedom is what you do with what's been done to you."

—Jean Paul Sartre

Any 12-step recovery program, including Al-Anon, has a fourth step that includes taking a self-inventory and outlining a blueprint of one's strengths and shortcomings. To get through emotional recovery, this step was necessary in order to have a baseline overview of who I am now. I continually evolve, so that baseline changes as I do. However, I need to know where I am now to determine where I want to go next in choosing who I want to be.

One of the most common symptoms of those affected by an abuser of substance, or any other kind of abuse, is becoming what is called a "codependent." Codependents have a strong need to control and be needed by others as a result of coping with dysfunctional, abusive relationships. Usually, dysfunctional enmeshment and dependency relationships are set up. This also results in the codependent being the responsible one while the "dependents" are irresponsible and needy.

Our need to control is so out of control that all kinds of imbalances exist in our lives. Blurred lines or no boundaries are established between self and relationships since we did not know any better. As women, we were raised to be the parent, yet we were still a child to our parent, who was irresponsible and abusive. We grew up knowing no other way, so when we start to "love" and date, we attract "takers" until we choose to learn and apply healthy boundaries.

I had to learn who I was in order to determine who I wanted to be. I asked myself, "Who am I? How do others see me?" Why was I giving yet not receiving love and care like I wanted and/or was giving in dating relationships? As I sought to expand my learning and awareness of self, I went to individual and group counseling, the Self-Awareness Institute weekend seminar and Al-Anon. Later, I discovered ACA's 12-step meetings.

Some resources cost money; others were free or based on donations, like the 12-step meetings. At Al-Anon, I learned about detachment to focus on improving myself, as I am the only one I have control of, and my outlook and perspective affects how I am treated by others. That outlook affects how I see what is going on around me, who I am attracted to and who is attracted to me. I learned that shifting my perspective is an "inside job."

In order to rebuild myself to whom I wanted to be, I realized that I needed to deal with my feelings of pain and suffering. These feelings slanted my perspective of people, and my assumptions and expectations for me with others. Some of these assumptions were so engrained that I thought that was just the way the world was. Although discouraging, I thought that relationships were just about me giving and someone else taking or abandoning, neglecting, or abusing me in some way, or simply not reciprocating in a flow of give and take.

I finally accepted that I had to deal with my feelings and heal my inner child to be free to interact with others and life the way I truly wanted. To deal with my pent-up anger, pain and sadness, and then get to acceptance and forgiveness, I found and chose the Self-Awareness Institute weekend seminar.

Dealing with anger head on leads to pain, sadness and grieving. Elisabeth Kübler-Ross talks about this cycle of grieving with death but also with changing (Kübler-Ross, 1969). This discussion helped with my understanding as grieving was part of my process.

I was grieving about:

- Not having had what I wanted as a child or as a young adult

- Choices I made out of ignorance that gave me more of what I didn't want in relationships

- Hardships I made for myself, not knowing any better

- Continuing to "fall down the pothole," and not understanding that I could choose to go around it and/or "go down a different street"

- My daughters, who had to be without the kind of father I truly wished for them because of my prior relationship choices

- Not getting it right the first time, even though I didn't know how or have any parenting or coaching to teach me better

- Why it took so long to figure out life management, create healthy intimacy, and make healthier parenting choices

Finally, I forgave myself and others, which led to acceptance and gratitude. I figured out a lot and have made many healthy and beneficial choices since my young adulthood. I have become happier with who I am as a parent, self, wife and contributor to my community.

The first breakthrough was to recognize my anger and deal with it head on in the Self-Awareness Institute weekend seminar, which was quite a process. One of the anger-releasing exercises was to beat a punching bag with a bat while yelling all of the things I wished I could have said to my abusers, and to keep doing it until I had it all out. Because I did it so loudly and for so long, the police came to the seminar door, having been called by outside bystanders who thought that someone was being beaten or killed. That has never happened before or since in that seminar.

As one can imagine, I had a lot of anger to release in that safe environment. Some say it takes a lot of courage to face ourselves, take ownership of our feelings and deal with them; however, when we don't, it blocks us or eats us alive. It takes a lot of energy to stuff down our feelings and not deal with them—energy that we could put to more constructive outcomes for ourselves when it becomes available.

Some of the ways we stuff down our feelings is by numbing them with drugs, alcohol and sex; being busy; overworking; oversleeping; overeating; isolating; and ruminating. This is done to avoid feeling and what we don't want to deal with, and prevents us from living life fully.

Brené Brown is a thought leader who teaches about the good kind of vulnerability, which allows us to have joy, love and connection in our lives. She has concluded that "Americans are the most over-medicated, drugged, over-weight and numbed-out population on the planet" (Ted Talks, Brené Brown, September 2012) because we are afraid to be vulnerable. We use self-protection and denial instead of self-revelation and connection to self and others.

To do that we have to be willing to face our feelings,

heal the inner child and release ourselves to constructive connection. Self-reflection and honesty lead to integrity. Integrity integrates connection.

Personal development leads to integrity and a good kind of willingness to be vulnerable to allow connection in our lives with self and others.

As I write this, I'm still finding more self-revelation that I didn't recognize. For example, by the time I was 17 years old, Mother had moved us 15 times. My mother was 37 years old when I was 17; she had been married six times and we had moved one to two times yearly. There was no real opportunity to form friendships. I played well with others, usually as a leader of neighborhood kids playing kickball or hide-and-seek. I tended to be a tomboy who did wheelies on a Honda 90 over the mudflats of Alaska, outside of Homer. Developing friendships occurred when I became older, on my own, and determined to stay in a location for years at a time.

Questions for Thought:

1. What feelings do I have most of the time- Mad, Sad, Glad or Fear?

2. Am I supported well?

3. Do I receive love and positive support often?

4. How much do I give versus receive "good"?

CHAPTER FIVE

WHO ARE OTHERS?

"We don't see things as they are, we see things as we are."

—Anaïs Nin

One of the good things my mother taught me was to be honest and straightforward and look people in the eye. In spite of the instability and different step-fathers coming in and out of our lives, we learned some positive life management skills from Mother in her more stable moments. However, when it came to friends, it just seemed easier to play by myself, when sporadic leisure time was allowed, or with my sisters. I don't remember any neighborhood children as friends. We usually lived in rural areas, which was Mother's preference. Day excursions to explore nearby parks were the most positive leisure activities we had as a family.

There was ignorance, so to speak, about different kinds of people, relationships, or how to know who was trustworthy or safe. Subsequently, while innocent and naïve, there were encounters with what I've learned are called "predators" (i.e., child molesters, rapists, and con artists) at home as a child and on my own in my young adult years.

Mother trained me to be the parent to care for my siblings, have responsibility for them and care for the house and sometimes cook. That pattern taught me how to be and give to others, but there was no training about how to assess others and/or protect myself from them when they turned out to be predators. Somehow, I instinctively managed to protect myself from any direct victimization, but I experienced exposure to predatory abusive actions, which caused confusion about who was safe and viable for a trustworthy relationship.

Mother was not dependably safe—emotionally or physically. Some of our step-fathers were protectors from Mother's behavior; others were predators themselves in different ways; some were a mixture of both. Understanding what love was or was not was very confusing. Love seemed abusing, being abandoned and/or neglected, and it became a two-edged sword or a velvet anvil. It was no wonder that the relationships I'd chosen for love intimacy gave me very mixed and some heartbreaking results. I decided to take a hiatus from intimacy and was determined to figure myself out. I wanted to change myself and my perspective so I could attract and have the kinds of relationships I really wanted. I was 34 years old.

After attending Al-Anon, and reading about recovery from codependent behavior, I realized that I was unaware of healthy boundaries. Reciprocity was not in my expectations in relationships. I'd been taught strongly about what I was to give.

Seeking self-help "how-to" resources became my mentors. Only by attending 12-step meetings at Al-Anon and ACA, reading *Codependent No More* (Beattie, 1987), studying John Bradshaw's work, learning about Myers-Briggs personality communication types, male speak versus female speak from John Gray and Ellen Kreidman (*Light Her Fire, Light His Fire* audio CDs, 1998) and developing networks of love, including support (De Angelis, 1995).

The *California Therapist* magazine (July/August 1990) published the following boundaries list:

Chapter Five

A CHECKLIST ON BOUNDARIES IN RELATIONSHIP

WHEN YOU GIVE UP YOUR BOUNDARIES IN A RELATIONSHIP YOU:	WHEN YOUR BOUNDARIES ARE INTACT IN A RELATIONSHIP YOU:
*Are unclear about your preferences	*Have clear preferences and act on them
*Do not notice unhappiness since enduring is your concern	*Recognize when you are happy/unhappy
*Alter your behavior, plans or opinions to fit the current moods or circumstances of another (live reactively)	*Acknowledge moods and circumstances around you while remaining centered (live actively)
*Do more and more for less and less	*Do more when that gets results
*Take as truth the most recent opinion you have heard	*Trust your own intuition while being open to other's opinions
*Live hopefully while wishing and waiting	*Live optimistically while co-working on change
*Are satisfied if you are coping and surviving	*Are only satisfied if you are thriving
*Let the other's minimal improvement maintain your stalement	*Are encouraged by sincere, ongoing change for the better
*Have few hobbies because you have no attention span for self-directed activity	*Have excited interest in self-enhancing hobbies and projects

*Make exceptions for a person for things you would not tolerate in anyone else/accept alibis

*Are manipulated by flattery so that you lose objectivity

*Try to create intimacy with a narcissist.

*Are so strongly affected by another that obsession results.

*Will forsake every personal limit to get sex or the promise of it

*See your partner as causing your excitement

*Feel hurt and victimized but not angry

*Act out of compliance and compromise

*Do favors that you inwardly resist (cannot say no)

*Disregard intuition in favor of wishes

*Allow your partner to abuse your children or friends

*Mostly feel afraid and confused

*Have a personal standard, albeit flexible, that applies to everyone and asks for accountability

*Appreciate feedback and can distinguish it from attempts to manipulate

*Relate only to partners with whom mutual love is possible

*Are strongly affected by your partner's behavior and take it as information

*Integrate sex so that you can enjoy it but never at the cost of your integrity

*See your partner as stimulating your excitement

*Let yourself feel angry, say "ouch" and embark upon a program of change

*Act out of agreement and negotiation

*Only do favors you choose to do (you can say no)

*Honor intuitions and distinguish them from wishes

*Insist others' boundaries be as safe as your own

*Mostly feel secure and clear

*Are enmeshed in a drama that is beyond your control

*Are living a life that is not yours and that seems unalterable

*Commit yourself for as long as the other needs you to be commited (no bottom line)

*Believe you have no right to secrets

*Are always aware of choices

*Are living a life that mostly approximates what you always wanted for yourself

*Decide how, to what extent, and how long you will be committed

*Protect your private matters without having to lie or be surreptitious

This list helped me gauge how I was functioning in relationships versus how I wanted to function in relationships, recognize what outcomes were showing up and picture what kind of relationships I wanted to thrive in.

The list also helped me assess who and what kind of behavior to attract from others and keep in my life and learn how to move past or away from the rest. Eventually I learned how to deal with difficult people and/or difficult behavior. I noticed that, although I had choice as to whom and to what behavior I kept in my inner circle of friends, I still had encounters with badly behaving people at work, at school, while shopping and with medical caregivers. Learning strategies from Sam Horn (Intrigue Agency) and her *Tongue Fu!*® and NAMI, in their free 12-week course on dealing with emotionally challenged loved ones, helped me to have ready strategies when confronting bad behavior from others.

The journey to learn about others took a long time and many experiences; however, it seems that this saying is true: "When the student is ready, the teacher shows up." Sometimes it's in the form of books, seminars, CDs, a movie, or a new friend or trainer. Reading books like *Never Be Lied to Again* (Lieberman, 1998) and *Social Intelligence* (Goleman, 2006) helped in this regard.

Questions for Thought:

1. How do I see myself?

2. How do I see others?

3. What are the patterns of relationships in my life?

4. What can I learn or do to have the lids of relationships I want?

CHAPTER SIX

WHO IS MY FAMILY?

"Like an unchecked cancer, hate corrodes the personality and eats away its vital unity."

—Martin Luther King, Jr.

John Bradshaw shares that dysfunctional family members play various roles in family dynamics (Bradshaw, 1995). These families have secrets about the abuse, and all members are sworn to secrecy, either overtly or covertly, so the face of the family often looks different than the real dynamics. My role as the oldest child was hero, placater, protector for my younger siblings, distracter and peacemaker—usually at a high cost to myself.

To others, my mother's behavior was outgoing, engaging and upbeat until or unless she was crossed or did not get her way; then, her rageful behavior was embarrassing. Because my siblings and I were so well behaved, it appeared that she was a good mother, whether she was single or married at the time, so her appearance to those who did not know her well was deceiving.

In the third grade, Mother set me on the hot wood-burning stove, on my bare bottom, as punishment. Whippings on my back and bottom became the focus because these bruises wouldn't show. The men she married did not know what to do about her behavior once they knew of it. Usually, Mother would do her abusive behavior when the husband was not at home.

There was ignorance and then denial. Sometimes, there was confrontation or the turn of a blind eye until divorce, or possibly a sudden separation with either parent leaving or Mother leaving and taking us with her. It became about survival and high-alert living for many years until I could live on my own at 16 and be a senior in high school.

As I mentioned in Chapter 2, I was home for a summer after graduating from high school when the Worcestershire Sauce "showdown" happened, which led me to be permanently on my own after that. Mother really was no longer involved in my life after I had a taste of living on my own. I could not and would not take any more of her rage and abuse. Mother was single again by that time. So who was my family? My siblings? What adults were there to model for or coach me? I knew that I had to figure life out on my own. I liked learning so I continued school and went to college.

In college I decided to study psychology, so I could learn about healthy behavior and the causes of unhealthy and/or destructive behavior. Communication courses were appealing. Learning about communication dynamics, feelings, self- assessment, sensing what others say and don't say, nonverbal communication, disclosures and withholds interested me. Transactional Analysis (TA) theory and self-analysis were introduced, and reading *Games People Play* (Berne, 1964) revealed non-straightforward ways people behave or interact.

The dysfunctional triangle racket of Persecutor–Rescuer–Victim, which is played out among people, was revealing. In other words, when one role is played by someone, that person will play the other two roles in the relationship dynamic or situation before the cycle dynamic is completed. It is generally repeated several times for an ongoing dynamic among people who are "playing" these roles. The results never lead to healthy outcomes.

From TA and this triangle, concepts are learned to identify others who relate cleanly and straight-forwardly versus those who are "gamey" (i.e., play rackets and games and are not trustworthy in that dynamic or behavior). The process of learning who to trust—and for what—started to reveal itself. No matter how healthy we behave, I learned from TA that no one is 100% trustworthy for everything.

As humans, we all have our strengths and short-comings. We learn to love those we love, given all of those characteristics, when those shortcomings are tolerable and safe enough for us. Therefore, part of healthy boundary setting is to assess who to trust for what, and then give when positive reciprocity is also in the dynamic.

With this realization, I was better able to make choices in relationships and determine what I received from them. My thoughts and observations affected who I was and the choices I made. I wanted "normal," harmonious, healthy relationships in my life. I learned that, for every situation or crossroad, there are at least five to seven options to choose from. This means that nothing we face has only two choices.

We're always at choice. We may not like all the choices or they may not be the ones we prefer, but there are always choices and we can choose. When relationship dynamics have been based on rackets and a triangle of Persecutor, Rescuer and Victim, those players don't easily relinquish their roles or easily let go of a player in that dynamic.

When one chooses to get well and require healthier dynamics for a relationship, there can be anger, backlash and much resistance from others. Sometimes those players have to be let go by the ones eeking wellness—sometimes temporarily and sometimes permanently. In *Unlimited Power* (Robbins, 1986), Tony Robbins reveals his need to change friends completely as he embarked and succeeded in making a new and better life for himself.

I discovered in Al-Anon and from other resources that, as we change to well-being, those around us may resist that change and try to hold us back. When pursuing well-being, we need to be persistent and determined for our own care first over the care of others. This is necessary to be self-caring and is not selfish.

Questions for Thought:

1. What role did I play in my family of origin?

2. How has that shaped who I am?

3. Who do I trust for what?

4. Am I trustworthy to myself? To others?

CHAPTER SEVEN

WHO CAN I BE?

"It's never too late to be what you might have been."

—George Eliot

L earning now that I "am at choice" (i.e. know that I can choose....)—who can I be? Who do I *want* to be? I'm more in control of my life than I thought! I can change myself and change my world.

In *Father Knows Best*, *The Waltons*, and *Bonanza*, I had models of parents and families that I could follow. I could look around and continue to "find and follow the Good." Fortunately, my mother attended church and took us to Sunday school and Confirmation, so I could pray and connect with a higher power. I learned to connect spiritually and knew that my maternal grandmother continued to pray for us, even though she did not know where we were.

Somehow, I was able to be led to positive models in spite of distresses in my life. Somehow, I was able to seek and find the positive. At one point, I became grateful for the hardships that drove me to Al-Anon and ACA. The distresses had gotten so bad that I sought help to change rather than cope with the way life was showing up for me.

It seems that a lot of people just cope rather than opt for change to get better or have better in their lives. It doesn't have to be that way. We can choose. There are always options. *"When we're ready and seeking, the teacher shows up."*

We're led to the perfect book, program, seminar, CD, or trainer. Learning about healthy relationships and boundaries led to learning how to treat myself first and then teaching others how to treat me. If I did not nurture and treat myself well, with expectations for good to come to me, how would others do the same? If I didn't learn to say no, or maybe negotiate reciprocating friendships and relationships, who was going to do it for me? *No one.*

I still wanted to be a giving and loving person; however, if that wasn't what I received in return, I learned to move on and/or stop giving. I learned that not everyone is going to like me or like what I did or do in the moment—and that's okay. It's normal. Mark

Twain said, "You can please about half of the people half of the time." I think that he was a wise man. Terry Cole-Whitaker wrote *What You Think of Me is None of My Business* (Cole-Whittaker, 1988).

Finally, the people-pleasing part of me became more in balance. I could receive rejection and criticism without taking them so personally. I could listen and determine if I needed to change something in me to enhance my well-being or my relationships, yet still be true to myself. I learned that I could give and take, and allow myself to be supported bit by bit. I could disentangle the crossed wires on what love really looked and felt like while being supported in dependable and predictable ways.

Healing the inner child was accomplished hrough seminars offered by the Self-Awareness Institute and SAGE, which no longer exists, along self-development books and motivational readings by authors such as Wayne Dyer, Jack Canfield, Mark Victor Hansen, Bob Proctor, Oprah Winfrey, Marianne Williamson, Louise Hay and Debbie Ford.

Brené Brown is a more recent thought leader who discusses vulnerability and how necessary the good side of vulnerability is in connecting with others in our lives, yet our culture is focusing on fear-based security needs. We are shutting down from being willing to connect with each other out of unnecessary overprotection and isolation.

As I changed and moved toward wellness, I encountered women who had been through various kinds of abuse as children. We talked and learned that our challenges and patterns were similar in overcoming our barriers and emotional gaps of intimacy, with those outcomes and varied time periods for recognizing that we gave too much. We also learned to balance our giving and required reciprocity in our relationships. We no longer had relationships that required only our giving. We stood firm until shift happened for ourselves and for others in our lives.

One woman named Mary lived with an incestuous father and a mother in denial until she could take it no more. Mary married an abusive husband and had children, and then put an end to the abuse from her husband. She found a different and supportive mate, support groups and friends, and became a seminar leader for self-healing spirit- connected consciousness development.

Another woman, Sunny, was incested by her brothers. She also had a complete role reversal when she became surrogate mother and caretaker in her family of origin because her mother became ill over a long period of time. After years of caretaking many others—including an active, alcoholic father—Sunny learned to take and receive, and to say "no," "maybe," and "later." She learned to take time for herself and is now the head of a mental health hospital department, supervising and training other staff. She has raised and supported three healthy children through private schooling while caring for her mentally challenged and cancerous husband. In spite of the odds, she and her children are healthy emotionally and succeed in outstanding careers.

Questions for Thought:

1. What positive models are available to me ?

2. What Good can I Find and Follow?

3. How do I want to treat myself?

4. How do I want others to treat me?

CHAPTER EIGHT

EMOTIONAL ATHLETE

"Stand Firm until Shift Happens."

—*Victoria Rei*

"Stand Firm until Shift Happens" takes a lot of courage, strength, stamina, endurance and commitment. Just like an athlete, determination and visualization of the desired result or outcome, training and practicing are required to cross the finish line. Emotional intelligence requires self-development skills.

"Success IQ = Emotional IQ + Social IQ"

Dan Goleman's book, *Emotional Intelligence* (1995), outlines emotional skills, including:

- Identifying and labeling feelings;

- Expressing feelings;

- Assessing the intensity of feelings;

- Managing feelings;

- Delaying gratification;

- Controlling impulses;

- Reducing stress; and

- Knowing the difference between feelings and actions.

The cognitive skills related to that include:

- Self-talk;

- Conducting an inner dialogue as a way to cope with a topic or challenge or to reinforce one's own behavior;

- Reading and interpreting social cues;

- Using steps for problem solving and decision making;

- Understanding the perspective of others and understanding behavioral norms; and

- A positive attitude toward life and self-awareness.

Behavior skills include:

- Nonverbal and verbal;

- Making clear requests;

- Understanding eye contact and facial expressiveness, tone of voice and gestures;

- Responding effectively to criticism;

- Listening to others; and

- Helping others.

In *Emotional Intelligence*, Goleman shares data to suggest that emotional intelligence can be as powerful, and at times more powerful, than intelligence quotient. In part five, he shows that crucial emotional competencies can indeed be learned and improved, if we bother to teach or learn them (Goleman, 1995, p. 34).

In other words, social intelligence and relationship skills require skills to interact with and relate to others. In *Social Intelligence* (Goleman, 2006, p. 331), social intelligence varies from emotional intelligence with social awareness, including:

- Primal empathy;

- Empathic accuracy;

- Listening;

- Social cognition;

- Social facility or relationship management;

- Synchrony;

- Self-presentation;

- Influence; and

- Concern.

Emotional intelligence is about self-awareness and self-management. Goleman talks about "Low Road" versus "High Road" roles or problem solving with these mental abilities:

- *Low Road roles*: Ignoring the invaluable roles of social intelligence

- *High Road roles*: Using higher functioning social intelligences to solve problems or relate to others

High road abilities, like social cognition, are used, but we also need Low road functions of synchrony and attunement, which is an empathic concern for the impulse of compassion. Social cognition is the ability to understand other people and how they will react to different social situations (Goleman, 2006).

These writings led to my understanding that, again, I can *choose* to develop my skills of managing my internal emotional well-being, actions and reactions to others.

I found additional resources from writings and seminars about consciousness development, learning and deciding to be the best that I can be beyond recovery from an abusive childhood. I discovered the Avatar Course, which teaches one to learn to de-label and put off judging and instead focus on learning and being open. *Change Your Questions, Change Your Life* (Adams, 2004) focuses on learner questions rather than judgmental questions when looking and dealing with others and/or situations.

Successes are defined individually and by groups subjectively; however, success is still what most of us want regardless of how we define it. Intelligence is defined as emotional intelligence combined with intellectual intelligence to be effective in life and work, which means to be successful in ways that we define success.

We need to be developed emotionally and internally and be able to be socially intelligent to effectively work and interact with others. Whether one's measure for success is based on money, quality of life, or the number and quality of support networks, it is clear that relationships are involved.

In spite of technology shaping us into individual silos of daily functioning, we can override our tendencies for silo isolation by remaining connected to others. We can build and maintain connection to our feelings and others through relationships. Our values are the basis from which we see others and shape our approach to solving problems and conflict. Not only are we at choice about whom we are and whom we will become, it is our responsibility to own whom we are and whom we become.

We create better solutions when we work with others from a basis of trust, faith and synergy. We can focus on our abilities and progress rather than challenges and barriers. We can focus on "can" versus "can't." We can choose to see the glass half full rather than half empty. Some say the only difference between successful people and others is that those who are successful feel the fear and do it anyway.

In *What Happy People Know*, Dan Baker outlines thoughts that are the basis of living life for happy people (Baker, 2003).

Abraham Lincoln said, "People are just as happy as they make up their minds to be." Lincoln and Baker capture the idea that what we think is what we are and, if we want to be happy, we can be by focusing on that and deciding to be happy.

It is recognized that the opposite of love is fear rather than hate, and that hate is just a derivative of fear.

Love-based thinking leads to faith, cooperation and successful collaboration, which then leads to sustainable solutions. It asks learner questions versus judgmental questions and is based on faith and confidence that solutions for the good of all will come forth. The value is based on finding win-win solutions.

Fear-based thinking usually escalates any problem or conflict and creates division and alienation. Resistive solutions are brought about by authoritarian control. Solutions usually are only for the one or the few at the top, which are called zero-sum outcomes or win-lose scenarios.

As human beings, we recognize that we are emotional, physical and spiritual beings. To be successful in whatever terms we define, balance and connection are made in all three of these areas. We can exercise and feed ourselves in healthy ways to care for our physical being; likewise, we can develop, exercise and surround ourselves with healthy emotional care. Those who choose to connect spiritually, recognizing the need for that aspect of beingness, usually get to well-being quicker and easier.

The 12-step programs recognize the need to connect with a Higher Power, as one may define that. These programs continue to be successful in helping millions of people become well in various kinds of recovery. When one becomes spiritually connected, acknowledging that part of themselves and their needs, the tendency is to become kinder and embrace nonjudgmental, love-based questions. (Being religious is not the same as being spiritually connected.) The focus is on cooperation and collaboration.

After realizing that we are at choice and can own who we are, we understand and realize that we can go forward to be the best we can be. We can keep learning and evolving in the process, even up to the end of our life. It's never too late to be who we might have been.

Questions for Thought:

1. Do I choose to learn better emotional skills?

2. What emotional strengths do I have? What more do I want to learn?

3. Who do I want to be? Fear based or Love based persona?

CHAPTER NINE

BEING MY OWN HERO

"Being noble is being better than before."

—Paraphrased Eastern proverb

"Values are the emotional rules by which a society organizes and disciplines itself. Without them, nations and individuals can run amok."

—James A. Michener

When I was kid, some of the recognized heroes were the Lone Ranger, Roy Rogers (and Dale Evans, his female counterpart), Wonder Woman, Superman and *Star Trek*'s Captain Kirk and Mr. Spock. In Greek mythology, heroes included Hercules, Zeus and Athena. Every culture and society has heroes with super strength and wisdom to solve crises quickly, even the most formidable ones. We are now facing formidable problems locally and globally in our everyday lives.

Superman was weakened and stripped of his power by Kryptonite. Emotional baggage does the same as it can derail us from success and stunt our development, keeping us from fulfilling our potential or being the best that we can be. However, when we choose to take the inner journey of self-development to increase and develop our emotional skills, we're taking the path of a hero. *We become our own hero.* We honor ourselves and feel good about who we are and how we handle our life.

Wayne Dyer shares an eastern proverb, which defines nobility as not being better than others but as being better than before (Dyer, 2010). As we choose to improve our emotional and social skills, we do become better than before. We are noble and display nobility. Once we have a handle on our inner emotional world, we see relationships with others differently. We become easier to get along with. Others become easier to get along with because there is more openness, understanding and willingness to trust ourselves and our insights. Relating to others from a basis of kindness versus a basis of fear changes the whole perspective and outcome of possibilities.

As we interact with others, we learn that there are many perspectives to lifestyle, culture, eating and working. It is educational to travel and see how differently clothes are washed, how food is cooked, or how houses are built. Language—even the same language—is spoken differently in different areas of a country.

Mansour Javidan, a professor at Thunderbird School of Global Management in Glendale, Arizona, developed a method of defining Global Intelligence and categorizing different communication, thinking and cultural styles in his assessment of executives of their Global Intelligence.

Different cultures around the globe are indirect communicators versus direct communicators. For example, Myers-Briggs self-assessment is a personality inventory and categorization method of understanding different thinking communication styles of individuals in the United States. The more we understand our differences, the more we can build bridges of cooperation. As we learn where the other person is coming from, and what his or her interest and motivation are, the easier it is to build trust.

In *The SPEED of Trust*, Stephen Covey writes how trust leads to successful agreements quickly, where distrust causes failure and/or, at the very least, major delays until trust to serve mutual interests can be established (Covey et al., 2008). Then, Covey wrote *Smart Trust*, where the distinction is different than distrust, naïve trust, or gullible trust. Here, real stories of real companies abound with the successes of remembering that most people are trustworthy (Covey et al., 2012). Treating the majority of consumers accordingly is for the greater good and leads to higher revenues. Customers enjoy being treated well, instead of like the 1% to 2% who misuse policies of returns, contracts, or other exchanges, in my opinion.

Penn Jillette, magician and comedian, was interviewed in 2012 by Piers Morgan. In that interview, Jillette pointed out that, because trust is so low in our culture, no one feels innocent anymore. We are all treated with levels of overabundant security rules and regulations because of the low percentage of those who are criminals or abusers of common decency. Raising trust is accomplished with a choice that we each make about whom we are now, whom we are going to be and how we are going to be with others.

Is our focus on building bridges or destroying them?

Julie is a single mother of three who worked through an abusive marriage and her own learning disabilities. In her determination to be well, she chose to leave drug abuse behind. She has an established, thriving business and raised her children success-fully on her own in spite of their choices of drug use while in their teens. All of her children, who are now adults, are clean and sober and leading produc-tive, healthy lives. The grandchildren are raised in a healthy living environment. Many dysfunctional family patterns are broken and reversed to healthy ones.

Tammy was raised by two alcoholic parents with frequent arguing and harsh discipline. Emotion-ally, neither her mother nor her father was available during childhood. Instead, role reversal took place and her mother trained all three daughters to take care of her, especially Tammy. After years of giv-ing and giving, Tammy decided that it was time to receive. She chose to set different boundaries with family and her adult children. She now has four generations of a higher functioning and supportive family, who all learned healthy values of reciproc-ity. Tammy stood firm until family resistance to her changes shifted to cooperation and healthy connec-tion.

Questions for Thought:

1. Who are my heroes?

2. What characteristics about them do I like?

3. How can I " Be Better Than Before"™?

4. What next steps can I take to be who I want to be?

CHAPTER TEN

DO YOU WANT TO BE YOUR OWN HERO?

"The more one judges, the less one loves"

—Honore de Balzac

When we choose to have a better life, we choose to learn self-development to enjoy the life we are creating. We understand that we want to be better. By changing ourselves, we change our lives. This impacts others, how we treat others and how they treat us.

I realized recently that all leaders only lead in part of their lives. At times, they have to follow, like the rest of us, and buy clothes, get services on their home or car and attend concerts. Followers actually lead sometimes, such as workers teaching newcomers on the job, showing someone else the ropes, or modeling how to solve a problem for their coworkers. Who we choose to be shows up as how we choose to be with others, whether we are leading or following.

A store clerk reminded me of a saying: "Who we

are and the choices we make when no one is watching demonstrate our true character and values." Who we are and how we live our lives are models to someone—oftentimes without even knowing it.

I remember visiting my aunt and uncle as a young adult. Without them or me knowing it at the time, they became a model for what I wanted in my life: stability, family, home and marriage. Years ago, I remember a young man, who was standing under a streetlamp, forlorn because my mother forbade us to date. This brief memory gave me a point of reference of devotion and being cherished.

We can look around and "Find and Follow the Good." When we're in the midst of hardship or trauma, it's hard to see. Sometimes, even when we can only reflect backwards, we can see the good and the gifts that come from that hard time.

When we become whom we want to be, whether we know it or not, we are a change agent—first for ourselves; then, as we change ourselves, for others.

Others are impacted by the ripple effect from our changes. Others in our lives, who don't care for the changes or choose not to change in the same way, may leave.

As we go towards well-being, others who are also well and on their way to wellness come into our life. Our support grows and increases as we choose well-being over dysfunction, and we choose others in our lives accordingly. We are a change agent just by insisting on being treated well and by doing the same with others. By choosing to build bridges for ourselves, we build bridges for others. We solve breakdowns more peaceably. We create empowerment for ourselves and others.

When enough of us do this, we can create a critical mass turning point. A commonly known concept called the "hundredth monkey effect" (Wayne Dyer calls it "Pi" (Dyer, 2010)) is the equation for critical mass. When well-being and high social skills solve problems peaceably from a base value of love and not fear, cooperation and "Smart Trust" become the norm rather than the frontier that it is now.

Having high emotional and social intelligence skills can create a base of "currency," if one uses business phrasing. Relationship currency is highly valued in business or public nonprofit sectors. In other words, one's network makes it easier to increase business and create positive results for projects. High emotional and social skills increase that currency exponentially and the results can be measured monetarily (Covey et al., 2008 and 2012). The paradigm is shifting. The critical mass turning point is getting closer.

Hillary Clinton said it best: "Where there has been more travel there is greater understanding. We are in competition for the future for customers and for influence. We'll either figure out how to be more integrated or we will disintegrate." (Doyle, September 2012).

Personal and social skill development is not just a nice thing to do. Self-development in emotional and social skills is a necessity. No one knows this more than those of us who were raised in harm's way as children. No one knows this more than those who've been bullied at school or at work, or have been the brunt of emotional violence. (Physical violence is also emotional violence.)

Oftentimes, we don't realize the gifts we have until

or unless we've experienced the opposite. That is the gift that comes from having had an abusive childhood. When we finally break through to healthy living and well-being, we know the difference and greatly appreciate it.

The *choice* and *determination* to get to a better place is what makes it happen. The paradigm is shifting in our country. The old authoritarianism is clashing with the demand for cooperation and collaboration as many cultures bring their perspectives to the world of living and work.

Cultural populations and worker demographics have changed, bringing their communication styles to the workforce. Multiple generations are in the workforce and the consumer population. If there was ever a need for higher emotional and social skills, it is now. Managers, project managers, case managers, law enforcement officers, restaurant workers, consumer goods workers, caretakers, factory workers, corporate executives and maintenance and cleaning workers all deal with others with different perspectives than their own. Having the ability to see through someone else's eyes, or walk a mile in their shoes, helps us know how to build bridges and collaborate to build a better today and tomorrow. Those who have had the opposite experience and have chosen to acquire skills of well-being make good leaders and followers.

My wish is for all of us to be the best we can be and to use high road social skills to solve problems and succeed in life. We can *choose* to be happy and offer this choice to others in whatever walks of life we lead.

Questions for Thought:

1. Who do I want to be? What do I want to do and have in my life?

2. Do I choose to be happy? And Be Better Than Before?

3. How will that change my life? And improve relationships around me?

4. What resources in this book will help me get there?

BIBLIOGRAPHY

"A Checklist on Boundaries in a relationship." *The California Therapist*, July/august 1990.

Adams, Marilee G. *Change Your Questions, Change Your Life*. San Francisco: Berrett-Koehler Publishers, 2004.

Baker, Dan, and Cameron Stauth. *What Happy People Know*. New York: St. Martin's press, 2003.

Beattie, Melody. *Codependent No More*. Center City, Mn: Hazelton Foundation, 1987.

Berne, Eric. *Games People Play*. New York: Ballantine Books, 1964.

Bradshaw, John. *Homecoming*. New York: Bantam Books, 1990.

———. Family Secrets. New York: Bantam Books, 1995.

Canfield, Jack, and Mark Victor Hansen. *Chicken Soup for the Soul*. Deerfield Beach, FL: Health Communications, Inc., 1993.

Canfield, Jack, et al. *The Success Principles*™. New York: HarperCollins publishers, 2005.

Cole-Whittaker, Terry. *What You Think of Me is None of My Business*. San Diego: Oak Tree Publications, 1988.

Covey, Stephen M.R., et al. *The SPEED of Trust*. New York: Free Press, 2008.

———. *Smart Trust*. New York: Free Press, 2012.

Cowan, Dr. Connell, et al. *Smart Women, Foolish Choices*. New York: Penguin Putnam, Inc., 1986.

De Angelis, Barbara. *Confidence: Finding It and Living It*. Carlsbad, Ca: Hay House, Inc., 1995.

Doyle, Kevin. *"Where in the World is Hillary?"* Condé Nast Traveler, September 2012.

Dyer, Dr. Wayne W. *The Power of Intention*. Carlsbad, Ca: Hay House, Inc., 2004.

————. *Inspiration*. Carlsbad, Ca: Hay House, Inc., 2006.

————. *Making the Shift* (audio CDs). Carlsbad, Ca: Hay House, Inc., 2010.

————. *From Ambition to Meaning* (audio CDs). Carlsbad, Ca: Hay House, Inc., 2011.

Ford, Debbie. *The Dark Side of the Light Chasers*. New York: Penguin Putnam, Inc., 1998.

————. *The Secret of the Shadow*. New York: HarperCollins, 2002.

Forward, Susan, et al. *Toxic Parents*. New York: Bantam Books, 1989.

Furman, Mark Evan, et al. *The Neurophysics of Human Behavior*. Boca Raton, FL: CRC press, 2000.

Goleman, Daniel. *Emotional Intelligence*. New York: Bantam Books, 1995.

———. *Social Intelligence*. New York: Bantam Books, 2006.

Gray, John. *Men Are from Mars, Women Are from Venus*. New York: HarperCollins, 1992.

Kreidman, Ellen. *Light Her Fire, Light His Fire* (audio CDs), 1998 www.lightyourfire.com).

Kritsberg, Wayne. *Adult Children of Alcoholics Syndrome*. Pompano Beach, FL: Health Communications, Inc., 1985.

Kübler-Ross, Elisabeth. *On Death and Dying*. New York: Touchstone/Simon & Schuster, 1969/1997.

Lieberman, David J. *Never Be Lied to Again*. New York: St. Martin's Press, 1998.

Oliver-Diaz, Philip, and Patricia O'Gorman. *The 12 Steps to Self-Parenting for Adult Children*. Deerfield Beach, FL: Health Communications, 1988.

Pelzer, Dave. *Help Yourself*. New York: Penguin Group, 2000.

Robbins, Anthony. *Unlimited Power*. New York: Ballantine Books, 1986.

Williamson, Marianne. *The Gift of Change*. New York: HarperCollins publishers, 2004.

RESOURCES

Alcoholics Anonymous
www.aa.org

Adult Children of Alcoholics (ACA)
www.adultchildren.org

Al-Anon
www.al-anon.alateen.org

Avatar Course
(consciousness development training)
Harry Palmer

Avatar Master
marilyn@avatarsv.com
408-378-9958
Marilyn Attebury

Brain Power On
www.brainpowercoaching.com
brainpoweron@cox.net
Don McKinnon
520-721-1266

Intrigue Agency/*Tongue Fu!*®
www.intrigueagency.com
andrew@intrigueagency.com
Sam Horn
703-475-9322

National Alliance on Mental Illness (NAMI)
www.nami.org

National Council on Alcoholism and Drug
Dependence, Inc. (NCADD)
www.ncadd.org

SAGE
(no longer in existence; self-development seminar)
Marilyn Attebury, practitioner

Self-Awareness Institute weekend seminar
(to heal the inner child)
www.selfawarenessweekend.com
Andrea Lambert, LMFT and founder
1-866-204-6384 toll free or 916-966-0411

TED talks
(studies on Vulnerability, Web/Internet)
Brené Brown, September 2012

Thunderbird School of Global Management
Glendale, Arizona
Mansour Javidan (2008) and Chris Pearson
(2010), professors

www.ingramcontent.com/pod-product-compliance
Lightning Source LLC
Chambersburg PA
CBHW060543100426
42742CB00013B/2430